...erihews of Paul Ingram

Paul Ingram

ICE CUBE PRESS, LLC, EST. 1993
North Liberty, Iowa

The Lost Clerihews of Paul Ingram

Paul Ingram

Illustrations by Julia Anderson-Miller

klĕr′ə-hyo͞o

______a

______a

_________b

_________b

The Lost Clerihews of Paul Ingram

Printed and Bound in the U.S.A. with recycled paper
1 3 5 7 9 8 6 4 2

Ice Cube Press, LLC (Est. 1993)
205 N. Front Street
North Liberty, Iowa 52317
319-594-6022
www.icecubepress.com • steve@icecubepress.com • twitter: @icecubepress

Front cover photo of author courtesy of Prairie Lights Bookstore.

ISBN 9781888160772

Library of Congress Control Number: 2014933251

The paper used in this publication meets the minimum requirements of the American National Standard for Information Sciences—Permanence of Paper for Printed Library Materials, ANSI Z39.48-1992.

Dedications

To Maurice Sagoff and G. K. Chesterton.
– Paul

For my husband Bruce, my dog Karlos and my mom, Mary, for always telling me to draw something.
– Julia

Paul Ingram

Used to finger 'em,

But now he does worse

He insults 'em in verse.

– Bruce Wheaton

Foreword

Anybody that has ever passed through Prairie Lights Bookstore knows that Paul Ingram possesses several kinds genius: he is, perhaps, the greatest reader and recommender who ever lived. Moreover, he is a genius of enthusiasm, and his methods of getting you to take a book home are a kind of hypnosis: he starts by magicking his hands across the shelves, *where's-the-book-where's-the-book*, he leaps from fiction to nonfiction in a spring-loaded fashion, he speaks to you in a voice that varies over octaves and decibels—a passionate shout, a seductive purr—he teasingly lifts the cover and shows you the jacket flaps. And that's only the *first* book. Before you know it you've bought six books, and somehow you don't mind. Paul Ingram hasn't *made* you buy that many books: he's recognized a need in you, and met it.

I imagine he has introduced more readers to their favorite books than any other bookseller. He has changed my life with books more than once: when I was graduating from the Iowa Writers' Workshop in 1990, getting ready to take the train from Mount Pleasant, Iowa, to Seattle, and then Seattle to Boston, I asked him for reading advice. He assembled a stack that included (among other books) Pete Dexter's *Deadwood*, Mary McCarthy's *Memoirs of a Catholic Girlhood*, and Alice Munro's *Friend of My Youth*, still three of my favorite books of all time. Two years later he gave me Rose Tremain's *Sacred Country*, which is the book I recommend more often than any other, and one I don't know if I would have found any other way. In 2001, he handed me a book that he loved and was sure I would love called *Observatory Mansions*. I hadn't heard of the author before (his name was Edward Carey), but I read the jacket copy and it convinced me, and as it happens, two and a half years later, reader, I married him.

Whenever I hear that someone is going to Iowa City, I tell them to stop by Prairie Lights—my favorite bookstore in the world—and then to ask for Paul Ingram—my favorite bookseller.

Sometime during these years I heard about Paul's poetry. Not from Paul, but from other people, at cocktail parties. The first one I heard was about Baudelaire (I won't quote it: you'll find it inside) and it made me snigger dirtily. It is still my favorite. Reader, if you and I were in a bookstore and I wanted to get you to read this book—and I do want you to read this book, I want to be a Paul Ingram and put a wonderful, life-altering book into your hands—I would open it up and start reading to you. Vincent Price! Ethel Merman! Charles Baudelaire, of course! You'd be sold immediately, which might disappoint me: these are poems meant to be read aloud.

Instead I will say: *The Lost Clerihews of Paul Ingram* are everything that Paul Ingram himself is: hilarious, ribald, tender, erudite, naughty, every decibel and every octave. More of his genius, in other words. You will love them.

—Elizabeth McCracken

Elizabeth McCracken is the author of the beloved novel *The Giant's House*—finalist for the National Book Award. She is also the author of *Thunderstruck & Other Stories; An Exact Replica of a Figment of My Imagination*; and *Niagara Falls All Over Again.*

Introduction

I started writing clerihews about twenty years ago. The process seemed involuntary, rather quick explosions bound by rhyme and form. I would speak a name and the rest of the poem would spill from me without careful thought. I was inspired by Canadian poet, rock critic, and musician, Opal Nations. His clerihew was, "Helen Keller/Had only a smeller/But through her teacher's zeal/Learned to talk like a seal." How are you not gonna like a little poem like that? The freedom of mocking the beloved. The dominance of rhyme and form over sense. The silliness of rhyme pushed to its snapping point.

The clerihew was first devised by English crime writer, E. C. (Edmund Clerihew) Bentley, who felt the limerick had fallen into disfavor with its nearly obligatory naughtiness. He invented a form, which he felt might be a more wholesome scheme for youngsters to play about with. Why he thought so, I do not know. Poets (W. H. Auden, Anthony Hecht) have done well with the form. But since the death of Bentley in 1956, the form has seldom been in use.

Mallarme
Had too much to say
He never quite
Left the paper white.

—W. H. Auden

The somewhat complex rhyme scheme is AABB. The first line must include the name of a well- or ill-known person. The second line must rhyme and mock. The second couplet should mock and further mock. The clerihews which took possession of me were of a particularly vicious strain. Clerihews which would have had Bentley quite upset. I do not do requests. The clerihews happen to me. I do not sit down to write clerihews.

The clerihew is a gesture of rhythm and rhyme not a statement of truth, and if Fuzzy Zoeller happens to rhyme with Helen Keller, both principals are fair game. If Mother Teresa's real name happened to be Spunt, the author of a clerihew would, obviously, be forced to point this out.

And how have they become lost? Many reasons. They are tiny and often find themselves on napkins, old receipts, sugar packets, and matchbook covers. No one keeps track of such ephemera. If the ephemera goes, the clerihew itself goes like the precious content of a dream. Sometimes even the subject is gone. If I go through old boxes of stuff, I find a few on a sheet of lined paper. This book exists because I found a mother lode of them in the basement: damp, discolored, disposable to a less sensitive eye than mine. This gave me enough material to make a book's worth.

To those offended by some of the clerihews in this book, I can only apologize, and ask the simple question, "Doesn't Whistler rhyme with fistula? Well, sort of?"

There are a couple of Ingram Clerihew characteristics that readers might particularly enjoy knowing. One is the tendency, with three-part names like Henry Wadsworth Longfellow, to simply drop the first part of the name. Call him Wadsworth Longfellow. Another enjoyable trick is to force a snobbish reader to mispronounce a name in order to have the joy of the rhyme. The French major must pronounce Baudelaire, Bodelair in order to rhyme it with "scrotal hair."

Carl Gustav Jung

Was impressively hung,

Which sorely annoyed

The good Dr. Freud.

Mario Lanza

Forgot the last stanza,

So he did a soft shoe

And sang poopoopadoo.

Margaret Mead

Used to fart when she peed,

A fact well known

To every Samoan.

Naguib Mahfouz

Had a passion for Jews,

He'd stroke 'em and nuzzle 'em

Quite odd for a Muslim.

Mark Rothko

Drove down to Costco,

For a barrel of gesso

And ten pounds of espresso.

Walker Evans

Could count by sevens,

He ate 49 hamburgers,

They said it was Asperger's.

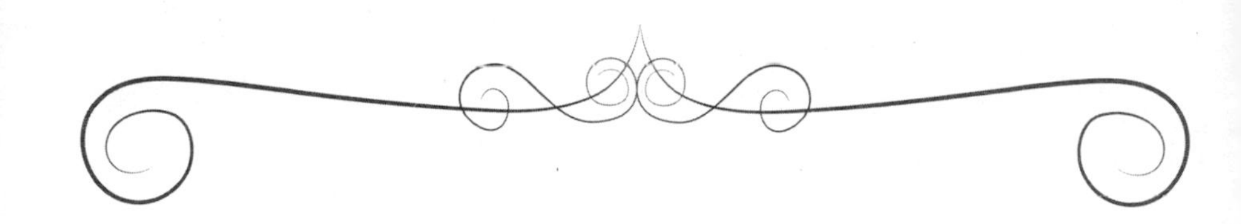

Charles Dickens

Had a thing about chickens,

He read chicken porn

To his precious Plorn.

Siegfried Sassoon,

While inhaling a prune,

Hollered, “Kyrie Eleison,

One hell of a raisin.”

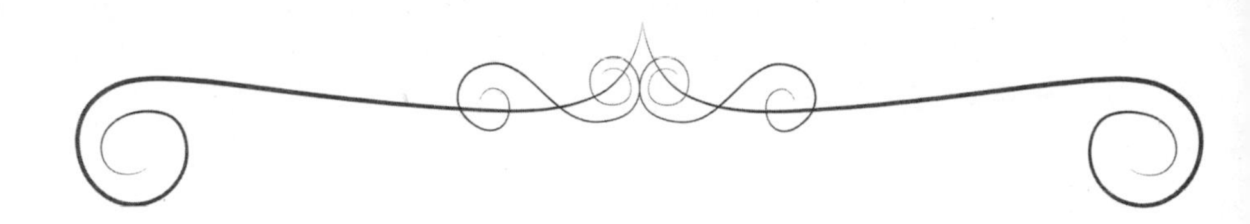

Charles Baudelaire

Picked at his scrotal hair,

And found a weevil

In his *Flowers of Evil.*

Forrest Gump

Told Donald Trump,

"You know I like you

We have the same IQ."

Henry Ford

Thanked the Lord,

Every day

For the T and the A.

Jeff Bezos

Believed he was Jesos,

He left out no detail

In dismantling retail.

Colonel Sanders

Often panders,

To the tasteless many

Just to make a penny.

Ignatius Loyola

Had a seed in his molar,

And, pray though he might,

It hurt him all night.

Simone Weil

Not known to smile,

A Christian mystic

Who was fond of brisket.

Washington Irving

Found unnerving,

The urge to wallow

In Sleepy Hollow.

Evelyn Waugh

Can stick in the craw,

Of the shy, the gentle,

And the sentimental.

Pierre S. du Pont

Could afford Vermont,

But was pleased with his share

Of Delaware.

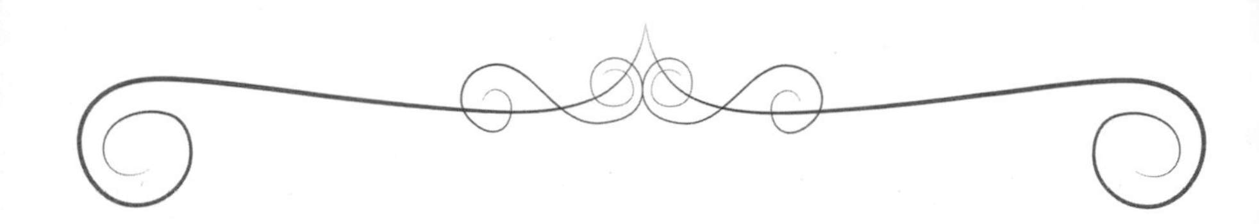

John Dunstable

Couldn't get comfortable,

In the Chapel Royal

On account of a boil.

Jonathan Franzen

Threw a tantrum,

When asked to go

On the Oprah show.

Martin Amis

Grew rich and famous,

Much to the disquiet

Of A. S. Byatt.

Rebecca West

Became obsessed,

With the nether smells

Of H. G. Wells

Vivian Vance

Put cheese in her pants,

Both Swiss and Havarti,

When she used to party.

Abel Gance

Dropped his pants,

And made a Napoleon

On the linoleum.

Glenn Beck

Was a red neck,

Who would get in your face

On religion and race.

Lionel Barrymore

While stroking his paramour,

Thought things would be special

If he also had Ethel.

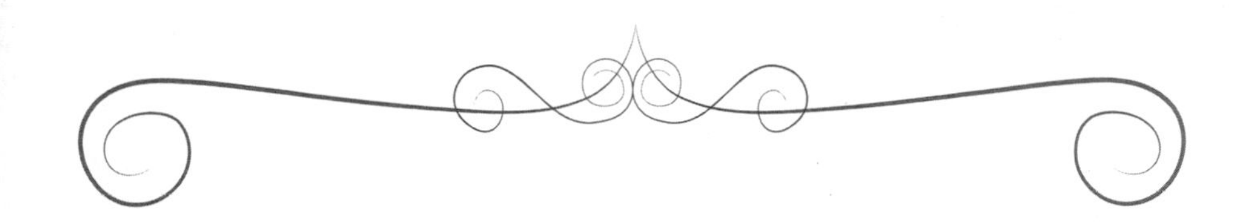

Igor Stravinsky

Couldn't convince me

He knew one damn thing

About the rite of spring.

Joesph McCarthy,

Hirsute and swarthy,

Never looked pretty

Before his committee.

Ivan the Terrible

Was truly unbearable,

Especially on the occasions

Of Tatar invasions.

Norman Rockwell

Used his cock well,

He used to boast

Of a Saturday Evening Post.

Willa Cather

Would really have rather

Been William or Walt,

Though it wasn't her fault.

Elmer Fudd

Was not a stud,

His only habit

Was to "Kill that wabbitt!"

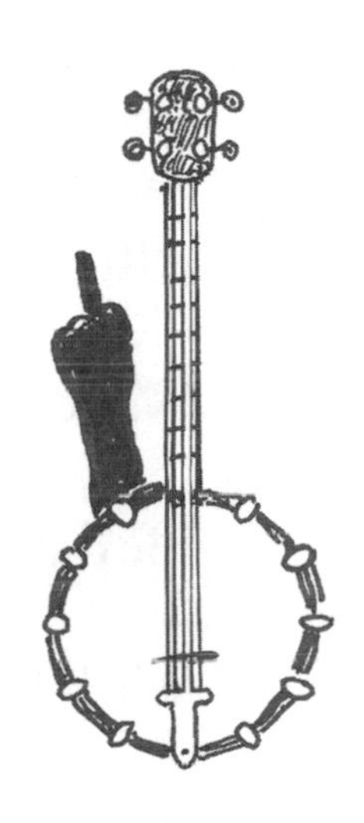

Earl Scruggs

Did not give hugs,

While Lester Flatt

Would stop and chat.

Alfred Lord Tennyson

Was crazy for venison,

He'd get stag and doe

With french fries, To Go.

John Milton

OD'ed on Stilton,

And lost his senses

With his amanuensis.

Andy Devine

And the Gadarene swine,

Had much in common

Around the abdomen.

Gustave Flaubert

Was seldom sober,

He wrote *Madam Bovary*

While in recovery.

Mamie Eisenhower

Had a drink twice an hour,

Thus the infamy

Of the overmatched Mamie.

Eleanor Roosevelt

Despised how her clothes felt,

After only one Scotch

They bound at the crotch.

Edward Abbey

Rugged and shabby,

Sat in the dark

At a National Park.

Sylvia Plath

Did competent math,

But lived for her tomes

Of unhappy pomes.

Jesus Christ

Was sliced and diced,

And punched with holes

To save our souls.

St. Francis Xavier

Watched his behaviour,

And never smoked dope

In front of the Pope.

George Berkeley

Looked through a glass darkly,

To find his breakfast cereal

Immaterial.

Thomas à Kempis

Drove down to Memphis,

A monastic spaceman

In the world of Graceland.

Sebastian Bach

Had a wen on his cock,

Said the good Doktor Steiner,

"This mass should be minor."

John F. Kennedy

Observed no amenity,

In having a go

At Marilyn Monroe.

Reverend Al Sharpton

Is an excellent marksman,

For the sake of his show

He'd like no one to know.

John James Audubon

Took too much laudanum,

And became unpleasant

With a ring-necked pheasant.

E. Allen Poe

Wrote a pome 'bout a crow,

As he finished his beer,

"Quoth the bird Everclear."

Walter Cronkite is

Subject to Bronchitis,

That being said,

He is also quite dead.

Anthony Burgess

Subverted his urges

With the ugly, mean,

Clockwork Tangerine.

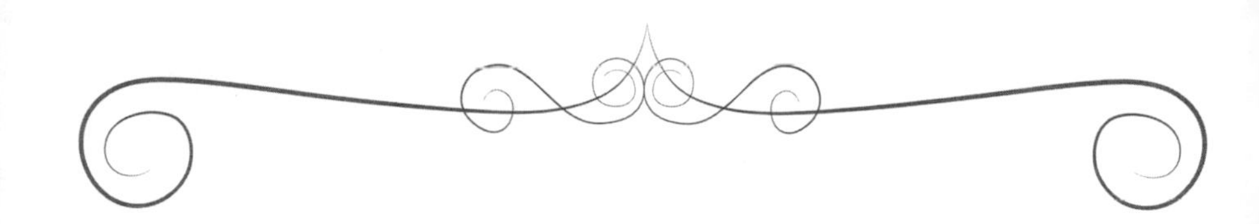

Ezra Pound

Could often be found

In black shirt cafes

Praising fascism's ways.

Janos Starker

Was a Nosy Parker,

He used to spy

On Zoltán Kodály.

Huddie Ledbetter

An inveterate bedwetter,

Wrote "Goodnight Irene"

On his bed of polystyrene.

Alice B. Toklas

Went smokeless,

A little hash

Under her moustache.

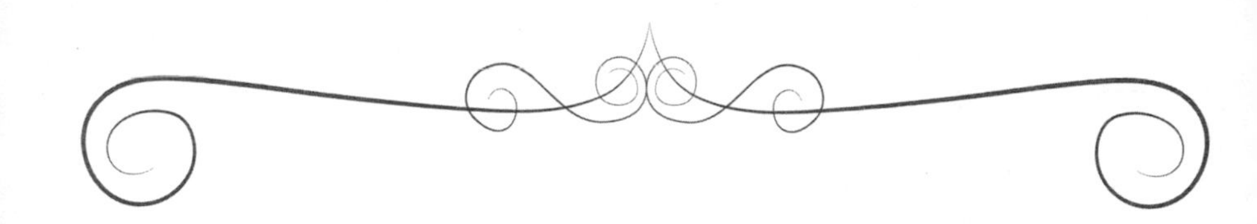

Euripides

Said, “Have a sip o’ dese,

Which do you like

The red or the white?”

Paul Auster

Said a pater noster,

Which, if you're a Jew,

You're not supposed to do.

John Irving

Had only one serving,

So he would feel great

At one fifty eight.

Edward R. Murrow

Had brows that would furrow,

As he'd squint through the smoke

At what might be a joke.

Bob Marley

When feeling gnarly,

Would roll up a joint

And thus he'd anoint.

Yehudi Menuhin

Earnest and genuine,

Was always smilin'

When he played violin.

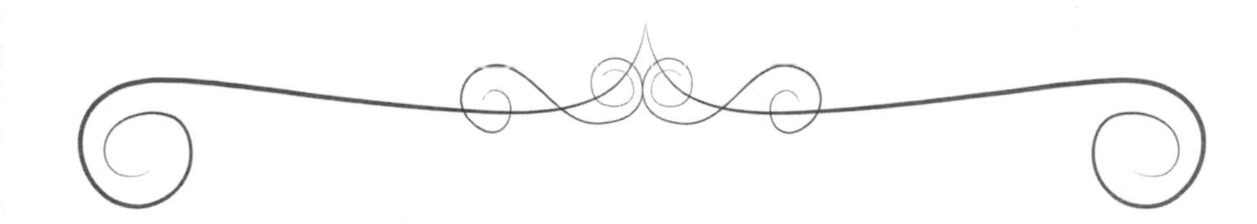

Lady Gaga

Could manage a raga,

But looked like a wanker

Next to Ravi Shanker.

Henry James

Did not chase dames,

His reputation

Was for observation.

Ring Lardner

Made fun of his gardner,

And underpaid

His upstairs maid.

Georgia O'Keeffe

In her personal fief,

Spent hours and hours

Drawing purple flowers.

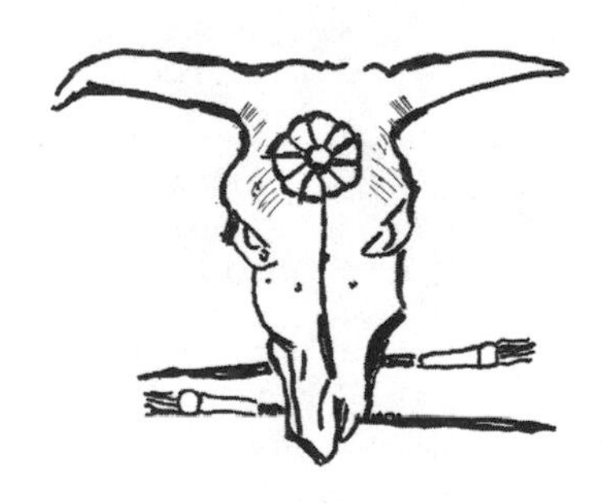

Kwame Nkrumah

Had no sense of humor,

The squirting flower

Left him looking dour.

Maurice Chevalier

Was perkier and jollier,

Though a bit less tall

Than Charles De Gaulle.

Pierre Boulez

Dit, “Faites ce que voulez,

Ça ne fait rien

À moi ni aux miens.”

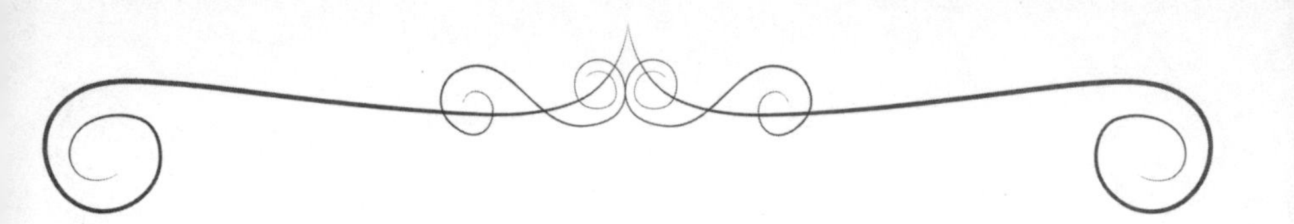

Anderson Cooper

Made nary a blooper,

But he liked to watch Fox

For the mismatched socks.

Senator Cruz

Never bothered to schmooze

Caught up in the immediacy

Of his own idiocy.

Immanuel Kant

Sang, "Plume de ma tante,"

Which gave him the stamina

For his prolegomena.

Marcel Proust

Liked Brussels sprouts,

But it was eatin' cookies

Got him writin' bookies.

John Keats

Had very few treats,

And a great deal of strife

In his short bleak life.

Agatha Christie

Would drink and get frisky,

She made quite a mess

On the Orient Express.

Ethel Waters

Went out with Porters,

Who paid her rent

As they came and went.

Theda Bara

Used dark mascara,

And her trademark crouch,

On the casting couch.

David Oistrakh

Went to the roicetrakh,

And lost a rubel

On the Daily Dooble.

Enzo Ferrari

Read *Huntsman, What Quarry?*

But had little to say

Of St. Vincent Millay.

Nelson Mandela

Was a wonderful fella,

But did not rate

With the Orange Free State.

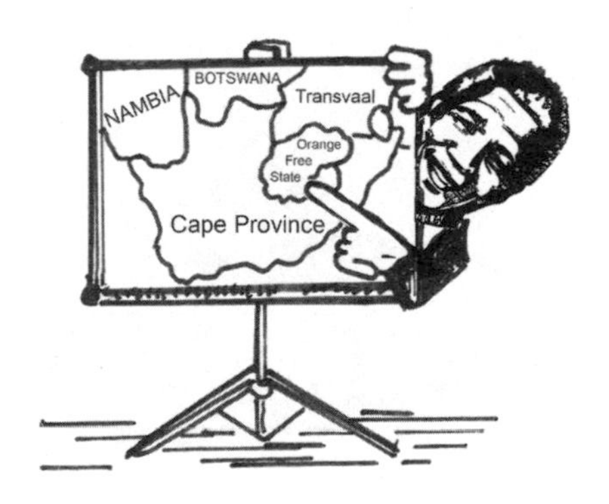

Sherman Alexie

Witty and sexy,

Brought smiles of elation

To the old first nation.

Rosa Parks

Did not read Marx,

But made her fuss

On a Birmingham bus.

Annie Oakley

Did pretty well locally,

But once she got around

She achieved some renown.

Vincent Price

Bit heads off mice,

To blunt the thrust

Of demon lust.

Georg Trakl

Lived a life of debacle,

Drugs and mania

And schizophrenia.

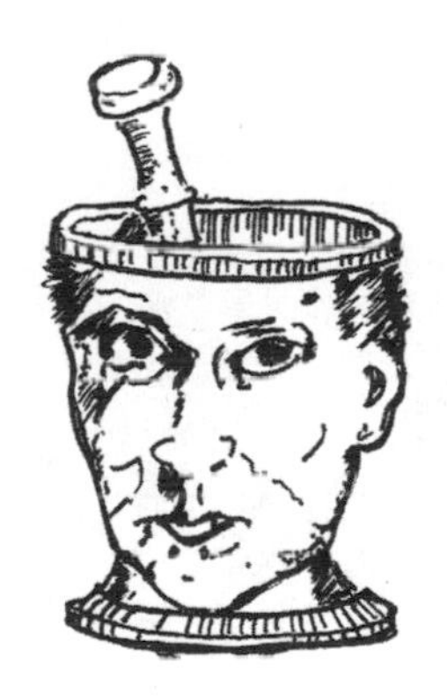

Marco Polo

Pleaded "nolo,"

After taking a minor

As a mistress to China.

Heinrich Schliemann

Found traces of semen,

That had long been frozen

In an ancient Trojan.

George Eliot

Read the *Iliad,*

Alone and in bed

With her melon-sized head.

Adrienne Rich

Though some called her bitch,

Was really okay

If you met her half way.

Martin Buber

Coughed up a goober,

Every time

He said L'Chaim.

Ben Bernanke

Reached for a hankie,

He was losing his nerve

At the Federal Reserve.

Harry Truman

Played beautiful Schumann,

But couldn't play stride

As hard as he tried.

Margaret Thatcher

Wouldn't play catcher,

So they used Judy Dench

To play Johnny Bench.

Edvard Grieg

Was minor league,

Though the *Peer Gynt Suite*

Is pretty neat.

Henry Purcell

Eschewed rehearsal,

For a more spontaneous

Dido and Aeneas.

Wadsworth Longfellow

Said, “You’ve got the wrong fellow,

I don’t care a turd’s worth

For you William Wordsworth.”

Hermann Hesse

Was OK at chesse,

But filled his needs

With little glass beads.

D. H. Lawrence

Wrote poems in torrents,

But he must have been dreamin'

It was really just semen.

Margaret Sanger

Drank a Harvey Wallbanger,

Which hindered her goal

Of birth control.

Mao Tse-tung

Said, "It tastes like dung,

If you don't cook

From my Little Red Book."

Louis Farrakhan

Was an Afro-American,

Who made the news

By baiting Jews.

Diana Ross

Knew who was boss,

She left The Supremes

To live with their dreams.

Britney Spears

Did not wear brassieres,

And cut off her hair

In the depths of despair.

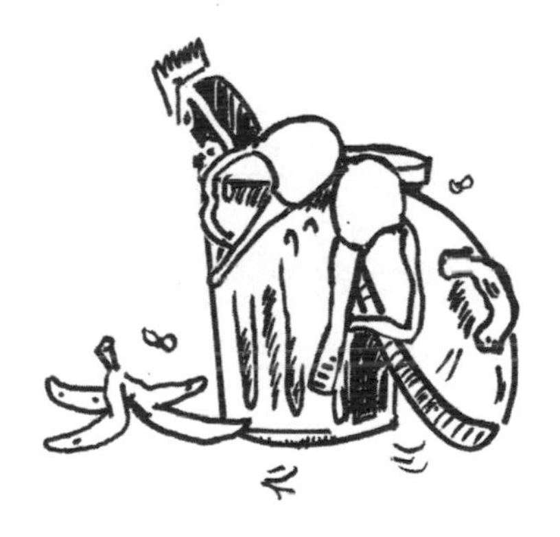

General Custer

Lost all of his luster,

And most of his pride

On his final ride.

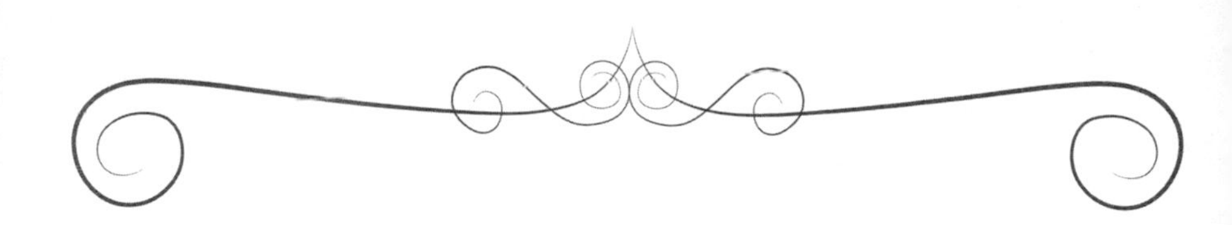

William McKinley

Disguised contempt thinly,

Which served to hasten

His assassination.

Greenleaf Whittier

Thought nothing was shittier,

Than being stuck in the snow

With Henry Thoreau.

William Whewell

Was a whiz in schewell,

Like John Stuart Mill

Whom he thought a pill.

Muriel Spark

Got bit by a shark,

A dank gory

Memento Mori.

Christopher Hogwood

Behaved as a dog would,

In committing rape

At The Maltings, Snape.

Helen Keller

Played Fuzzy Zoeller,

With a handicap of four

Though she should have got more.

Babe Zaharias

Played many and various

Past times and sports,

In men's under shorts.

Dubya Bush

Had a brain like mush,

But could fly a plane

with that worthless brain.

Miley Cyrus

Contracted a Virus,

That got her twerking,

Even when she was working.

Jean Sibelius

Used an alias,

He always checked in

As Huckleberry Finn.

Frank Lloyd Wright

In spite of his height,

Was the glittering jewel

Of the Prairie School.

William Faulkner

Had a dog and liked walking her,

When she got frisky

He'd have a whisky.

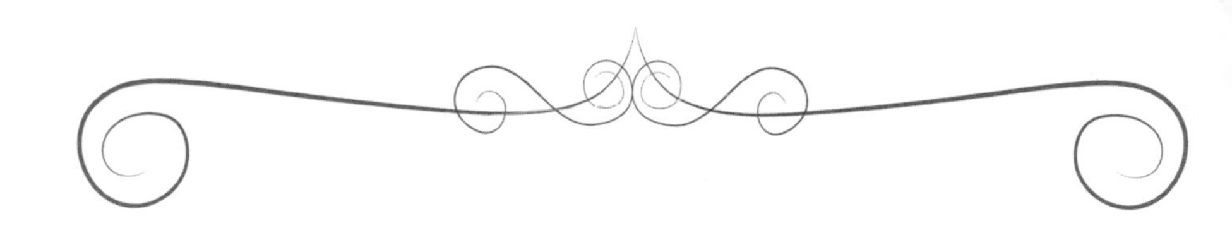

Leontyne Price

Was frightened of mice,

They'd crawl up her sleeve

When she'd recitative.

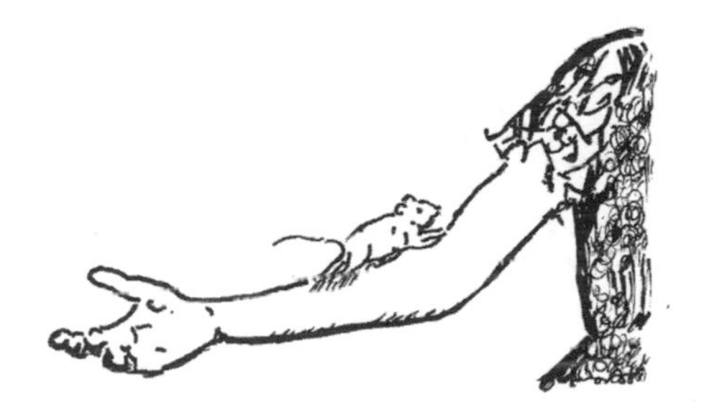

Ralph Abernathy

Was full of empathy,

He used to get weepy

At the NAACP.

Ferlin Husky

Played Sandusky

Holiday Inn

When pickings were thin.

Michael Jackson

Looked Anglo-Saxon,

Due to some nasty

Rhinoplasty.

Diana Spencer

Was top-rank at Mensa,

And won all her quarrels

With the overmatched Charles.

Ethel Merman

Got rid of vermin

By singing Cole Porter

For an hour and a quarter.

Mother Teresa's

Amniocentesis

Was performed by God

With a wink and a nod.

R.K. Narayan

Was a vegetarian,

A sirloin steak

Caused his knees to quake;

A rasher of bacon

Set his karma to shakin',

A cutlet of veal

Made him holler and squeal;

A Thanksgiving Turkey

Made him twitchy and jerky,

Southern fried chicken

Gave his tummy a lickin';

Barbecued ribs

Made him mean to his sibs,

Filet Mignon

Made him suffer alone:

It was all just carrion

To R. K. Narayan.

INDEX

G

H

I

J

K

L

M

N

O

P

R

S

T

V

W

X - Z

ACKNOWLEDGEMENTS

To author and sales rep, Bruce Joshua Miller (and Eric Miller who long ago ran a few clerihews in *Midwest Bookseller*) who had the vision and maintained it. To publisher Steve Semken who laughed at them and said, "I'll publish them." To the talented, energetic painter and illustrator Julia Anderson-Miller for illustrations and design. To publisher and mentor Elisabeth Sharlatt, who introduced me to the work of Maurice Sagoff, and who let me know that a book of Clerihews was not a dumb idea. To Mike Chasar, author of *Everyday Poetry*.

To my wife Ellen, who said, "That one is just not funny," on many occasions. To Bruce Wheaton and Ed Folsom, who liked them and wrote them too and made a wonderful game of it. To Garrett Stewart who egged us on mercilessly. To Chris Merrill and Charity Grant who told me they were funny long after I thought so. To Geoff Hope, who contributed the last couplet to Charles Baudelaire, and who helped with anything French.

Oscar Wilde
Married and fathered a child
Which proves, you might say,
he was not "toujour gai"

—Maurice Sagoff

To the staff and customers of Prairie Lights who had to listen to me fine tune, in a loud voice, for an unconscionably long period of time. To Prairie Lights for providing an environment full of so many names that they simply exploded from my mouth. To W. H. Auden *il miglior fabbro* (duh). To my grandchildren Erin, Lillian, and Sam, who make everything fun.

FURTHER PRAISE FOR *The Lost Clerihews of Paul Ingram*

Paul Ingram's
Cerebrum's
Made portable criticisms
Into pocket-sized witticisms.

—D. A. Powell, poet, *Useless Landscape, or a Guide for Boys: Poems*

Paul Ingram's lost clerihews are devilishly clever; Julia Anderson-Miller's illustrations are a wicked delight. The sum is much greater than its parts. Like BBQ and beer, a perfect pairing.

—Linda Bubon, Women & Children First
Chicago, IL

Paul Ingram is an extraordinary bookseller who has not only found the lost clerihews; he has elevated the entire form. This book forever shall reside in our guest bedroom so that visitors will either know or wonder what sort of people we are.

—Richard Howorth, Square Books, Oxford, MS

This is an essential addition to your clerihew library. Move over, E. Clerihew Bentley!

—Amelia Gray, author, *Threats*

A biographical (and very silly) four line poem is a clerihew. Thank goodness Paul Ingram found his lost clerihews because they are a book lovers delight! Hopefully this is just volume one!

—Anne Holman, The King's English Bookshop,
Salt Lake City, UT

continued

PRAISE FOR ***The Lost Clerihews of Paul Ingram continued***

A worthy descendent of the work of the English journalist who invented the form … I recommend happily.

—Lewis Turco, author, *The Book of Forms: A Handbook of Poetics*

Ingram's mischievous creations have been found at last ... and readers will soon enjoy the pleasure of their company.

—Robert Gray, *Shelf Awareness*

The Lost Clerihews of Paul Ingram is a reader's delight. Paul Ingram has for decades been one of the keenest readers and booksellers in the United States. If a reader cannot wander in to Prairie Lights to partake of Paul's wit and wisdom a reader can pick up a copy of *The Lost Clerihews of Paul Ingram* and get a sense of Paul's exquisite erudition.

—Paul Yamazaki, City Lights Booksellers, San Francisco, CA

Also from Ice Cube Press

The Miracle Boy
Patrick Irelan
19.95 • 9781888160765

Living with miracles is not as easy as people think. A boy walks on water, but that's perhaps the simplest miracle of all in this collection of engaging short stories full of both everyday and far out miracles. Some real, some hopeful. Love and travel, as well as wit and humor spice these tales of wishful wonder.

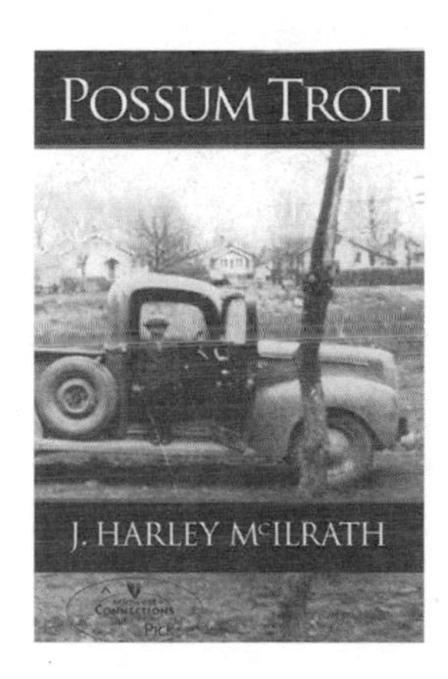

Possum Trot
J. Harley McIlrath
16.95 • 9781888160475

The pieces in this collection form a lament for a way of life mostly gone. "The family farm is dead. Did you know?" says one character within. "E.B. White writes *Charlotte's Web* today, it takes place in a hog confinement. Imagine Wilbur living in a concentration camp for pigs."These pieces, this Possum Trot, form not a lament, but a celebration of life. There is laughter here, the laughter that comes after the funeral, when the family is gathered in the home, the casseroles have been eaten and the boys are playing catch in their church clothes. The men have taken off their jackets and rolled their sleeves, and the women are pouring coffee. "Do you remember when…?" someone says. They do remember, and they laugh. There are tears in their eyes because one of the family is missing. But those tears are mixed with tears of laughter, because look around you. Here we all are. Still here. Alive and kicking.

The Ice Cube Press began publishing in 1993 to focus on how to live with the natural world and to better understand how people can best live together in the communities they share and inhabit. Using the literary arts to explore life and experiences in the heartland of the United States we have been recognized by a number of well-known writers including: Gary Snyder, Gene Logsdon, Wes Jackson, William Pitt Root, Patricia Hampl, Greg Brown, Jim Harrison, Annie Dillard, Ken Burns, Kathleen Norris, Janisse Ray, Craig Lesley, Alison Deming, Richard Rhodes, Michael Pollan, Dan Menaker, and Barry Lopez. We've published a number of well-known authors including: Mary Swander, Jim Heynen, Mary Pipher, Paul Engle, William Stafford, James Hearst, Bill Holm, Connie Mutel, John T. Price, Carol Bly, Marvin Bell, Debra Marquart, Ted Kooser, Stephanie Mills, Bill McKibben, and Paul Gruchow. We have won several publishing awards over the last twenty-one years. Check out our books at our web site, join our facebook group, follow us on twitter, visit booksellers, museum shops, or any place you can find good books and discover why we continue striving to, "hear the other side."

Ice Cube Press, LLC (est. 1993)
205 N. Front Street
North Liberty, Iowa 52317-9302
steve@icecubepress.com
twitter @icecubepress
www.icecubepress.com

Fenna Marie
Said to Laura Lee,
"We're really impressed
With that Ice Cube Press"